# Turandot / Aida

Happy House

# About Wise & Wide

- A systematic 6-level English reading program based on Lexile® measures
- Diverse and interesting topics chosen from the elementary curriculums of Korea and English speaking western countries
- Well-written books in various forms including fiction stories, descriptive texts, and classics retold
- The informative but original fiction stories grab your interest, leading to the easy and clear understanding of the educational content.
- Improve thinking skills with solid after-reading activities at all levels of the series.

**Wise & Wide** is a 6-level English reading program that consists of 60 books and each level is systematically divided by Lexile® measures. The Lexile® Framework for Reading is the most popular reading measuring system in American formal education curriculums and many English programs. Over 20 out of 50 states in the U.S. mark Lexile® measures directly on students' final report cards and over 300 well-known publishers adopt and use Lexile® measures.

Experience many kinds of readings written by professional writers from the U.S. and England. They used interesting topics that were carefully chosen after analyzing elementary curriculums from around the world including Korea, the U.S., England, and Australia among many others. Comprehensive after-reading activities including graphic organizers, speaking tasks, and After-reading Tests are ready for you.

### Levels in the series and their corresponding Lexile® measures

| Level | Lexile® measures | U.S. Grade |
| --- | --- | --- |
| Level 1 | Below 200L | Pre K - K |
| Level 2 | 190L - 400L | Lower Grade 1 |
| Level 3 | 350L - 530L | Upper Grade 1 |
| Level 4 | 420L - 650L | Grade 2 |
| Level 5 | 520L - 940L | Grade 3 - 4 |
| Level 6 | 830L - 1070L | Grade 5 - 6 |

* Smart Readers: Wise & Wide level 1 is applicable to the preschool level in the U.S.

* The source of the relationship between Lexile® measures and U.S. school grades: CCSS(Common Core State Standards) FOR ENGLISH LANGUAGE ARTS, APPENDIX A (2012, which is used by 45 states in the U.S.)

# Topic List

| | Level 1 | Level 2 | Level 3 | Level 4 | Level 5 | Level 6 |
|---|---|---|---|---|---|---|
| **Book 1** | Science>Biology: The hibernation of animals Story | Science>Biology: Living and nonliving things Story | Science>Biology> Animals & the Environment: Sea otters Story | Environment> Living with nature: The diver & the persimmon tree Story | Science>Biology> Animal: Amazing animals of the Amazon Story | Science>Biology: Germs, transmitted diseases Story |
| **Book 2** | Literature> World classics: Aesop's fables Story | Literature> Traditional fairy tale: Old tales about stones Story | Social Studies> Economy: To run a business to make and save money Story | Science>Biology> Plants: Photosynthesis Story | Science>Earth science: Earth's layers,earthquakes, volcanoes, and earth's atmosphere Report | Mathematics> Sequence: The golden ratio & the Fibonacci sequence Story |
| **Book 3** | Science>Physics: How shadows are formed Story | Literature> World classics: Peter Pan Story | Science>Scientific technology: Nanobots Story | Literature>Myths: World's creation stories Story | Literature> Legend: The story of King Arthur Story | Literature>Myths: Constellation myths Story |
| **Book 4** | Literature> Traditional literature: The Talmud Story | Science>Biology> Animal: Polar bears Story | Science>Biology> Animal: Mountain gorillas Story | Social Studies> Cultural anthropology: Amazing ancient cultures of the world Story | Science> Earth science: Clouds and weather Story | |
| **Book 5** | Social Studies> Ethics: Rules in daily life Story | Science>Biology : The five senses Report | Social Studies> Cultural anthropology: Astonishing festivals Report | Art>Music: Stories from two operas Story | Social Studies> World culture & history: The Renaissance Story | |
| **Book 6** | Social Studies> World geography & travel: Tourist attractions around the world Story | Science>Biology> Animal: Dinosaurs Story | Science> Astronomy: The solar system Story | Social Studies> People: Three great people who overcame hardships Story | Science>Scientific technology: The wonderful world of robots Report | |
| **Book 7** | | | | Science & Social Studies> Technology & culture: Inventions from around the world Report | Art>Works of art: Famous paintings Report | |
| **Book 8** | | | | | | |
| **Book 9** | | | | | | |
| **Book 10** | | | | | | |

* 10 books in each level will be published.

# How to Use This Book

## •Before Reading

You can easily find the topic and what kind of story you are about to read.

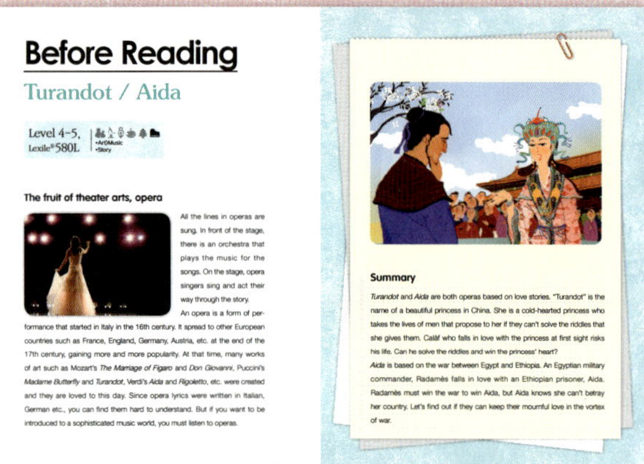

## •The text

All the stories were written by professional writers from the U.S. and England, so you will read authentic and appropriate English sentences and expressions in every book in the series.

## •Pop Quiz

Check out right away if you understand what you have just read by solving a pop quiz that checks your comprehension.

## •Key Words

The key words and expressions on each page are listed for you to easily study them.

## •Aha! Tips

Download free Korean explanations at *www.ihappyhouse.co.kr* for all of the sentences marked with "Aha!". These explain cultural, scientific, and economic knowledge or they deal with aspects of English such as grammatical structures or idiomatic expressions. There are lots of "Aha! Tips" to help you understand the text.

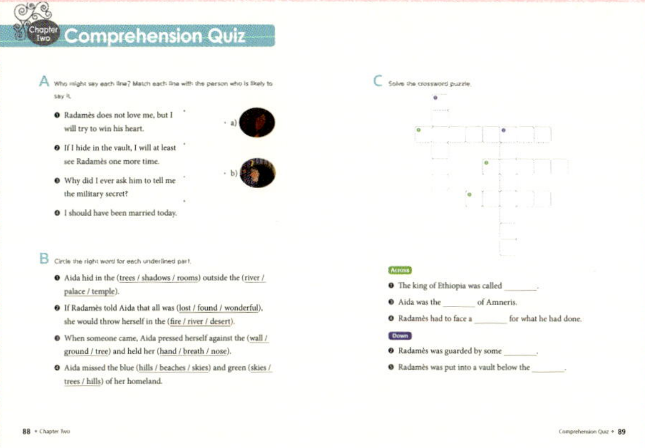

### •Comprehension Quiz

After reading one chapter, solve various questions to find out if you fully understand the content.

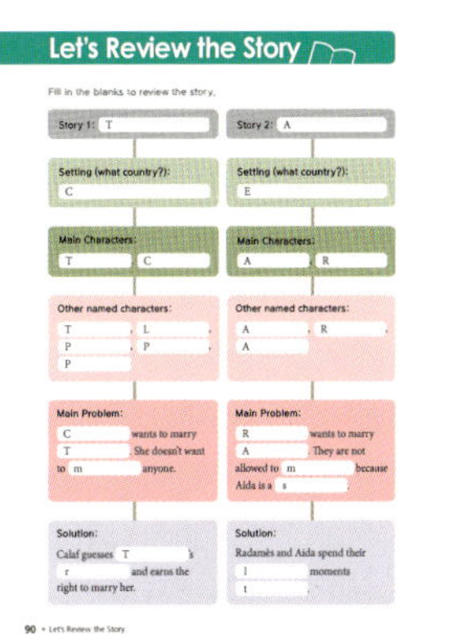

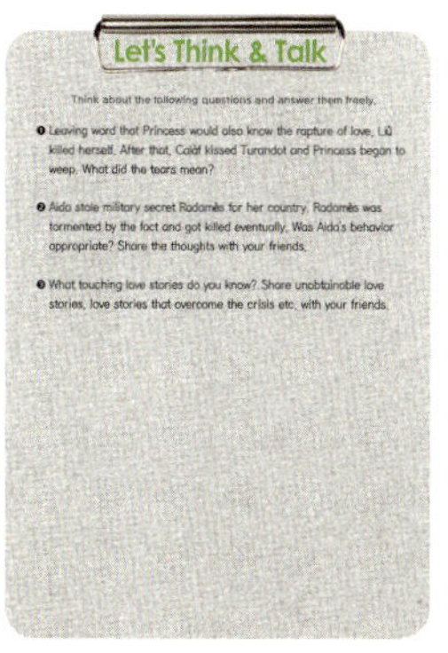

### •Let's Review the Story /
### •Let's Think & Talk

Fill in the blanks in the organizer to summarize the whole story. Express your own thinking and feelings about the story by answering the questions. You can build up logic and reasoning skills for your essay examinations in the future.

## Appendix

### Audio CD

In the CD audio book form, the texts are read vividly by American professional voice actors.

### After-reading Test

Solve an additionally provided After-reading Test for each book.

### The Korean translation, Answer Keys, a Word Quiz, a Word List, and Aha! Tips for each book

You can download them for free at *www.ihappyhouse.co.kr*

# Before Reading

## Turandot / Aida

Level 4–5, Lexile® 580L

•Art)Music
•Story

### The fruit of theater arts, opera

All the lines in operas are sung. In front of the stage, there is an orchestra that plays the music for the songs. On the stage, opera singers sing and act their way through the story.

An opera is a form of performance that started in Italy in the 16th century. It spread to other European countries such as France, England, Germany, Austria, etc. at the end of the 17th century, gaining more and more popularity. At that time, many works of art such as Mozart's *The Marriage of Figaro* and *Don Giovanni*, Puccini's *Madame Butterfly* and *Turandot*, Verdi's *Aida* and *Rigoletto*, etc. were created and they are loved to this day. Since opera lyrics were written in Italian, German etc., you can find them hard to understand. But if you want to be introduced to a sophisticated music world, you must listen to operas.

## Summary

*Turandot* and *Aida* are both operas based on love stories. "Turandot" is the name of a beautiful princess in China. She is a cold-hearted princess who takes the lives of men that propose to her if they can't solve the riddles that she gives them. Calàf who falls in love with the princess at first sight risks his life. Can he solve the riddles and win the princess' heart?

*Aida* is based on the war between Egypt and Ethiopia. An Egyptian military commander, Radamès falls in love with an Ethiopian prisoner, Aida. Radamès must win the war to win Aida, but Aida knows she can't betray her country. Let's find out if they can keep their mournful love in the vortex of war.

# Contents

# Turandot / Aida

# Turandot / Aida

# What is Opera?

An opera is a play, often with three or more acts. Each act has different scenes that tell a story.

It has actors in costume, and stage sets that show where the action is taking place.

However, the unique thing about an opera is that everything is set to music.

The actors are singers — often the best in the world.

All the words are sung, rather than spoken, and they are accompanied by an orchestra.

The words of an opera are called *libretto*.

Many people think an opera is difficult to understand.

This is because often the words are in another language.

Some of the most famous operas are written in Italian or German. Also, the style of music might not be what you are used to.

However, if you know the story behind the opera, it is much easier to understand.

Then, it becomes an exciting musical adventure!

In this book, you will read the stories behind two famous operas: *Turandot* and *Aida*.

The music for *Turandot* was written by an Italian composer called Giacomo Puccini. He was born in 1858, in a large family of seven children.

▲ Giacomo Puccini

The Puccini family was very musical. Puccini's father, grandfather and great-grandfather wrote music and were well known in their hometown.

Puccini wrote several operas, and *Turandot* was his last one.

He died in 1924, leaving *Turandot* unfinished and another composer, Franco Alfano, completed the opera.

The music for *Aida* was written by another famous Italian composer called Giuseppe Verdi. He was born in 1813 and received his first lessons in composing music at school.

Verdi wrote many operas before completing *Aida* in 1871. He wrote 26 operas in total.

▲ Giuseppe Verdi



**Which country were Puccini and Verdi from?**

ⓐ Germany

ⓑ Italy

**KEY WORDS**

- musical
- adventure
- composer
- great-grandfather
- write music

- well known
- unfinished
- complete
- in total

# Turandot

(Written by Giacomo Puccini)

# The Cruel Princess

Long, long ago, in the Chinese city of Peking, a servant stood outside the Imperial Palace.

He called out in a loud voice to anyone who would listen.

"Hear the command of the Princess Turandot. Anyone who wishes to marry her must correctly answer three riddles."

The crowd murmured excitedly.

The princess was incredibly beautiful, and many men wanted to marry her.

"But," went on the servant, "anyone who fails to answer the riddles will die."

Everyone gasped. They knew that the Princess Turandot was a cold-hearted woman, but this was too much!

**KEY WORDS**

| | | |
|---|---|---|
| • cruel | • command | • incredibly |
| • Peking | • correctly | • go on (go-went-gone) |
| • servant | • riddle | • fail |
| • Imperial Palace | • crowd | • gasp |
| • call out | • murmur | • cold-hearted |
| • in a loud voice | • excitedly | • be too much |

What about the handsome Prince of Persia? They all knew that he had been seeking marriage with the princess. He had already tried to answer the riddles. What would happen to him now?

As if he knew their thoughts, the servant shouted some terrible news.

"When the moon rises tonight, the Prince of Persia will be killed."

Some of the people were excited at this, and they began to shout.

"We will have entertainment tonight," one of them said.

Others were horrified. Among them was a young servant girl named Liu.

Her master, an old man called Timur, stood with her.

**What time of day will the Prince of Persia be killed?**

ⓐ when the sun rises
ⓑ when the moon rises

**KEY WORDS**

- What about...?
- Persia
- seek
- terrible
- entertainment
- horrified
- master
- push past
- get a good view of
- execution
- knock
- push...aside
- be in danger of
- trample
- step
- shadows
- lift

As the sun set, more and more people pushed past,
wanting to get a good view of the prince's execution.
Timur was knocked to the ground, and nobody stopped
to help him.
Liu tried to help him up, but it was too difficult.
People pushed her aside, and Timur was in danger of
being trampled.
"Help me, someone, please!" called Liu.
A young man stepped out of the shadows. He was tall
and strong, and he lifted Timur from the ground.

The two men looked at one another, amazed.

"Father?" said the younger man. "Is that really you?"

"Calaf, my son!" Timur's eyes filled with tears.

He had not seen Prince Calaf for a long time, since he was chased away from his throne in the kingdom of Tartary.

Chinese rulers had taken over that country, and they wanted to make sure that its king and prince never returned.

If Timur or Calaf were found by their enemies, they would be killed.

"Hush!" said Calaf, pressing his finger to his lips. "You must not say my name aloud.

Men are still hunting for me, as they are for you. We must keep our identities secret."

Liu stood back, her head bowed in respect as the two men talked.

But Timur took her elbow. "Do you remember Liu, my servant?

She is the only one who has remained faithful to me."

Calaf smiled at Liu and bowed to her.

"Why have you been such a faithful servant?" he asked.

Liu blushed. She could not tell him the reason why.

What if he laughed at her?

"Come, don't be shy," said Calaf, kindly.

"One day, many years ago, you smiled at me," said Liu, dropping her head so that he could not see her face.

**KEY WORDS**

- one another
- amazed
- fill with
- chase away
- throne
- kingdom
- ruler
- take over (take-took-taken)
- make sure
- enemy
- press
- hunt for
- keep...secret
- identity
- bow
- in respect
- remain
- faithful
- blush
- What if...?

A pale light washed over the crowd. "The moon has appeared in the sky!" someone called.

Silence fell as the Prince of Persia was led out. He was only a young man, handsome and kind looking.

He bowed his head and allowed himself to be led before the executioner.

"Have pity on him!" shouted Calaf. "He does not deserve to die."

Other people raised their voices around him, calling for mercy.

Trumpets sounded, announcing the arrival of Princess Turandot.

Calaf gasped. He had never seen her before, but the stories about her beauty were all true!

**KEY WORDS**

- pale
- wash over
- appear
- silence
- **fall** (fall-fell-fallen)
- **lead out** (lead-led-led)
- allow oneself to
- executioner
- have pity on
- deserve to
- raise one's voice
- call for
- mercy
- trumpet
- announce

His heart beat faster as he watched her take her place in front of the palace.

He hoped that she might look his way and smile.

"So this is how it feels to be in love," he thought.

But Turandot did not look at Calaf. Her face was cruel and cold.

Despite the cries of the crowd, she lifted her arm to command the executioner.

He lifted his axe and waited for the signal.

Calaf couldn't think properly.

He was lost in his own thoughts and so desperate to speak to the princess that he shouted out her name.

Three times he called: "Turandot! Turandot! Turandot!"

At the same moment, she brought down her arm and the executioner brought down the axe.

The Prince of Persia cried out as the axe struck his neck.

Then there was silence.

Calaf's cries were drowned out by the voices in the crowd. Everyone was talking about Turandot's cruelty.

He looked around wildly. The princess was leaving!

**KEY WORDS**

- beat
- take one's place
- be in love
- despite (= in spite of)
- cry
- axe
- signal
- properly
- lost
- desperate
- shout out
- bring down
- cry out
- strike (strike-struck-struck)
- drown out
- cruelty
- wildly

He might never see her again, and then how would she know that he loved her?
On the palace steps there stood a huge gong.
When a man struck the gong, it meant that he wanted to marry the princess.
If he could only reach it and strike it, then everyone would have to stop and listen.
Calaf left Timur and Liu behind, though they begged him to forget his madness.
He pushed his way through the crowd until at last he reached the gong.
Just as he lifted the beater to strike it, three men jumped in front of him, blocking his way.
"No, sir!" said Ping.
"Please don't do it!" said Pong.
"Too much blood has been spilled already," said Pang. 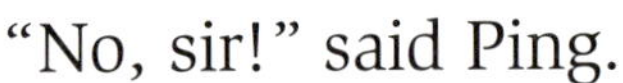

"We are the servants of the princess," they said.

"We have seen what happens to those who wish to marry her," Ping begged.

"My son, please stop!" Timur's frail voice called out.
Calaf turned around and saw his father struggling to
climb the steps. Liu was at his side, helping him.
He shook his head and raised the beater again.
"I must declare my intention to marry the princess," he
said.
"I beg you to think again." It was Liu, tugging at his
sleeve, her eyes glistening with tears.
"You are throwing your life away and I cannot bear the
thought of you dying."
"But why?" said Calaf. "You are just my father's servant,
and I barely know you."

Liu lowered her head and her voice was only a whisper. "Because I love you, Prince Calaf."

Calaf knew what it felt like to be in love. But all he could think of was Princess Turandot.

He shook off Liu and, with all his strength, struck the gong.

# Comprehension Quiz

**Chapter One**

**A** Circle the right word for each underlined part.

**❶** The command was read out by a (servant / prince).

**❷** The (servant / princess) was incredibly beautiful.

**❸** Liu was a (princess / servant) of Timur.

**❹** Calaf was a (prince / princess) from another country.

**B** Fill in each blank with the right conjunction below.

| as | but | though | and |
|---|---|---|---|

**❶** Liu tried to help him up, _______________ it was too difficult.

**❷** The princess was incredibly beautiful, _______________ many men wanted to marry her.

**❸** Calaf's heart beat faster _______________ he watched Turandot arrive.

**❹** Calaf left Timur and Liu behind, _______________ they begged him to forget his madness.

**C** Choose the best answer to each question.

**❶** Why did Liu blush when Calaf spoke to her?

    a) She had never met him before.

    b) She did not like him.

    c) She was in love with him.

    d) She could not speak his language.

**❷** How did Calaf declare his intention to marry Princess Turandot?

    a) He shouted at her.

    b) He played her some music.

    c) He asked her servants to speak for him.

    d) He struck a gong.

**D** Mark T for true or F for false.

**❶** The Prince of Persia was an old man.  T  F

**❷** Princess Turandot did not look at Calaf.  T  F

**❸** The Prince of Persia was silent when the axe struck him.  T  F

**❹** Princess Turandot was not as beautiful as people said she was.  T  F

# The Secret Name

The next morning, Ping, Pong and Pang were awake long before sunrise.

They sat together in the palace talking about Turandot, and about the men who had tried to win her heart.

"What can we do?" they wailed.

"More blood will be spilled before this day is over. Who can stop her terrible reign?" said Ping.

As sunlight crept into the sky, the palace trumpets sounded.

It was time for the riddle ceremony to begin.

The same crowd gathered again, this time enjoying the warmth of the morning sun.

**KEY WORDS**

- secret
- awake
- sunrise
- win one's heart
- wail
- reign
- **creep** (creep-crept-crept)
- ceremony
- warmth
- cheer
- bravery
- stranger

When Calaf stepped out onto the palace steps, all the people cheered.

Many people had heard of his bravery.

They wanted to see if this handsome stranger could make the princess love him.

"It is impossible!" they declared.

## POP QUIZ

**Why did the people cheer when Calaf appeared?**

ⓐ They knew that he was brave.

ⓑ They hoped that he would die.

Turandot's father, the emperor himself, sat on his throne
in front of the palace.

Even he begged Calaf to walk away from this challenge.
"You will never answer her riddles," he said. "You will
be dead before the day is over."

Calaf shook his head. "I love her, and I would rather die
than live without her."

Princess Turandot walked out in front of the crowd. She held her head high, but her eyes were cold.

Calaf watched her eagerly but she never once looked at him.

Instead, she began to tell the story of her ancestor, Princess Lou-Ling.

"Princess Lou-Ling was murdered by a prince who came to try and conquer our land," she announced.

"That is why I have turned against all men, and none of them shall ever own me." 

**POP QUIZ**

**What happened to Princess Lou-Ling?**

ⓐ She married a man that she did not love.

ⓑ She was murdered by an enemy prince.

**KEY WORDS**

- emperor
- walk away from
- challenge
- would rather A than B
- eagerly

- ancestor
- murder
- conquer
- turn against
- own

At last, Princess Turandot turned her gaze on Calaf.

"Here is the first of my three riddles," she said. "Think carefully before you answer."

The crowd went quiet.

"What is born each night and dies at dawn?"

All kinds of thoughts went through Calaf's mind. A baby could only be born once, not each night.

It must be something else.

When he had gone to bed the night before, he had found himself hoping that perhaps Turandot might love him. But that morning, when daylight flooded the sky, he realized that she probably never would.

That was it! That was the answer!

**POP QUIZ**

**What did Calaf think of when he went to bed?**

ⓐ his fear of death
ⓑ his hope for Turandot's love

**KEY WORDS**

- turn one's gaze on
- dawn
- daylight
- flood
- realize

- still
- feather
- clap
- sterner

"Hope," he said, in a clear voice so that everyone could hear.

The crowd was so still that anyone could have heard a feather falling.

"Correct," said Princess Turandot.

"Hooray! He was right!" People began to clap and shout.

"What is the next riddle?"

Princess Turandot did not clap or shout. She did not even smile.

Instead, she looked sterner than ever.

"What flickers red and warm like a flame, yet is not fire?"

Calaf thought hard. Something red and warm. Could it be the sun, when it set in the evening sky?

He glanced at Turandot's face.

A red dot had appeared in each of her cheeks, where the blood rushed to her face.

That was it! That was the answer!

"Blood," he said.

Princess Turandot's cheeks flushed redder and she trembled.

"You think you are so clever, but you will never guess the answer to the third riddle.

What is like ice, yet burns?"

Calaf looked toward the crowd, hoping that someone might shout out a suggestion.

He had no idea what the answer could be.

Something so cold that nothing could melt it, and yet it could hurt people.

His eyes slowly lifted towards Turandot.

She stared at him coldly, but her eyes danced as though she could not wait to punish him.

"Turandot!" he announced.

The crowd gasped. Of course!

## POP QUIZ

What gave Calaf a clue to the second riddle?

ⓐ the sun
ⓑ Turandot's face

**KEY WORDS**

- flicker
- flame
- glance at
- rush
- flush

- tremble
- guess
- suggestion
- melt
- hurt

- stare at
- coldly
- as though
- cannot wait to
- punish

They began to cheer and dance.

This handsome man would not die after all, and neither
would any more men after him.

But something strange was happening to Princess
Turandot.

She seemed to crumple and fall. She even looked as
though she might begin to cry.

She turned to her father, the Emperor. "Please don't
make me marry this man," she begged.

"He is a stranger to me."

Prince Calaf, who really did love Turandot, could not
bear to see her so distressed.

"Let me tell you a riddle," he suggested. "If you fail to
answer it correctly, then you must marry me.

But if you can find out the answer, then I will die, and
you will be free."

"Yes, yes!" said Princess Turandot, eagerly. "Tell me the
riddle."

"Very well, then." Prince Calaf looked directly at her and
said, "What is my name?"



**KEY WORDS**

- after all
- crumple
- fall
- cannot bear to
- distressed
- find out
- directly

That evening, Calaf went for a walk in the palace
garden.

Now that he had earned the right to marry the princess,
he was allowed to wander there as he pleased.

The air smelled sweet with the scent of flowers.

But what was that voice calling out in the distance?

It was another royal messenger.

He declared that nobody in Peking would sleep until the
princess learned the name of the stranger.

"None shall sleep," Calaf said to himself, "yet they still
won't know my name.

I will have victory over this princess."

Ping, Pong and Pang came rushing out into the garden.

"Please withdraw your offer and leave the city," Ping
pleaded.

**KEY WORDS**

- **go for a walk** (go-went-gone)
- **now that**
- **earn**
- **right**
- **be allowed to**
- **wander**
- **as +** *subject* **+ please**
- **scent**
- **in the distance**
- **royal**

- **messenger**
- **have victory over**
- **rush out into**
- **withdraw**
- **offer**
- **plead**
- **burst into** (burst-burst-burst)
- **arm**
- **dagger**
- **threaten**

"The princess has declared that everyone in Peking will
be killed if she does not learn your name."

"I cannot," began Calaf.

But his voice was almost drowned out by the sound of
the crowd gathered outside the palace.

A group of men burst into the garden, armed with
daggers.

"Tell us your name," one man threatened, "or we will
kill you ourselves."

What was Calaf to do? If he refused to tell his name, the
men would kill him.

But if he did tell them his name, Princess Turandot
would be able to answer the riddle.

Then, Calaf would die anyway.

At that moment, some soldiers dragged in Calaf's father,
Timur, and the servant girl, Liu.

"You were seen talking to these people," one of the
soldiers declared. "Perhaps we can persuade them to tell
us your name."

The royal trumpets sounded, and Turandot entered the garden.

"Well?" she said to the soldiers. "Have you found out his name yet?

Perhaps the old man knows."

The soldiers raised their daggers threateningly towards Timur.

"No!" shouted out Liu, faithful to her master. "Only I know the name of this stranger, but I will not tell."

Princess Turandot ordered that Liu must be punished, but she still refused to tell the name.

"How does this woman stay silent?" asked the princess.

Liu, barely able to stand after the beating she had received, looked at her.

"Love," she declared. "It is love that makes me strong."

Princess Turandot shrieked in fury, and ordered that Liu be beaten again.

Calaf could not stand by any longer.

He made a move to help her, but Liu was afraid that he would get himself killed.

"Love," she murmured, as she seized a dagger from one of the guards.

What did the people in the crowd do when Liu killed herself?

ⓐ They cheered.
ⓑ They cried.

**KEY WORDS**

- barely
- beating
- shriek
- in fury
- beat (beat-beat-beaten)
- stand by
- make a move
- seize
- guard
- kill oneself
- stillness
- weep
- gather up
- funeral procession
- grief
- take away

"You too will know the joy of love, Princess." Then she killed herself with the dagger.

Stillness fell on the gathered crowd, broken only by the sound of people weeping.

Liu's body was gathered up by the soldiers. The people formed a funeral procession.

Full of grief, they followed her body as it was taken away.

Calaf and Princess Turandot were left alone. "You are the Princess of Death," snarled Calaf.

He grabbed hold of Turandot and pressed a kiss onto her lips.

The princess, who had never been kissed before, began to weep. 🕮 Aha!

"Even after everything I have done, you can still treat me so? Tell me your name."

Calaf, realizing that the icy princess was beginning to thaw, told her his name.

And so Calaf took his place on the throne next to Princess Turandot.

As she presented her new husband to the crowd outside the Imperial Palace, her voice trembled.

"I have learned the stranger's true name," she said. "His name is Love."

**KEY WORDS**

- leave … alone
- snarl
- grab hold of
- treat
- icy
- thaw
- take one's place
- present

# Comprehension Quiz

**A** Circle the right word for each underlined part.

❶ Calaf (died / smelled / walked) in the palace garden, enjoying the scent of (Turandot / flowers / Peking).

❷ Nobody would be allowed to (sleep / eat / marry) until Turandot discovered Calaf's (wife / history / name).

❸ The soldiers threatened to (kill / release / respect) Timur, but Liu was faithful to her (master / husband / self).

**B** Fill in each blank with the right adverb below.

| coldly | carefully | eagerly | correctly |
| --- | --- | --- | --- |

❶ Calaf watched the princess ______________, but she never once looked at him.

❷ The princess told Calaf that he must think ______________ before he answered.

❸ She stared at him ______________, but her eyes danced.

❹ If Turandot fail to answer Calaf's riddle ______________, she must marry him.

**C** Choose the best answer to each question.

❶ Why wouldn't Liu tell Turandot Calaf's name?

a) She did not want him to die.

b) She did not know his name.

c) She did not want Calaf to marry Turandot.

d) She did not want to be beaten any more.

❷ Why didn't the princess kill Calaf when she learned his name?

a) She had forgotten their agreement.

b) She was not strong enough to kill him.

c) She realized how much he loved her.

d) She thought that it was not his real name.

**D** Put the sentences in order.

❶ Some soldiers came into the garden.

❷ Calaf was in the palace garden.

❸ A group of men came into the garden and threatened to kill Calaf.

❹ Ping, Pong and Pang came into the garden and asked Calaf to leave.

________ → ________ → ________ → ________

# Aida

(Written by Giuseppe Verdi)

# A Great Victory

Thousands of years ago, the Pharaohs ruled the land of
Egypt. 

In the city of Memphis stood the royal palace.

Outside the palace, two men were having an urgent
conversation.

"The country of Ethiopia is preparing to attack us
again," said the high priest, Ramfis.

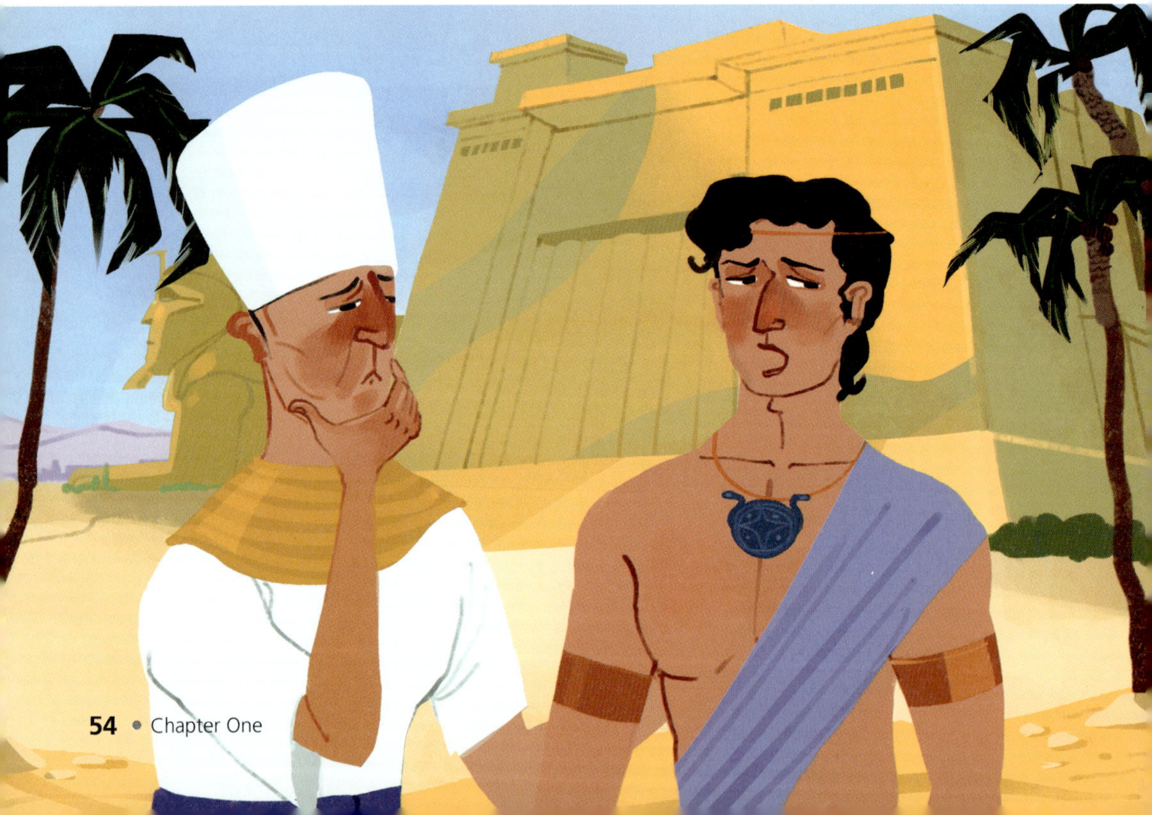

"They are already making their way along the valley of the River Nile. We must defend ourselves!"

"And so we shall," replied the young warrior, Radamès. "I hope that I shall be chosen as the commander of the troops. Then I shall lead them to victory."

There was another reason that Radamès wanted to win this battle. He smiled to himself as he thought about the woman he loved, Aida.

She was an Ethiopian woman who had been captured by the Egyptian army in a previous battle.

Now she was a slave, belonging to the Egyptian princess, Amneris.

**KEY WORDS**

- pharaoh
- Egypt
- Memphis
- royal palace
- urgent
- conversation
- Ethiopia
- priest
- make one's way
- defend
- warrior

- **choose** (choose-chose-chosen)
- commander
- troop
- battle
- slave
- Ethiopian
- capture
- Egyptian
- previous
- belong to

Everything was so difficult.

Radamès could not declare his love in public. Nobody would allow a slave to marry a warrior!

But he hoped that if he could lead the army to victory, then he might be able to free Aida and marry her.

"If only my dream might come true," he said to himself.

"An army of brave men with me as their leader, and the true prize will be my sweet Aida."

But things were even more complicated than that. The princess Amneris herself was in love with Radamès. She watched him all the time, knowing that he loved someone else.

Who could it be? Who would steal the heart of the man she loved?

Each time she and Radamès met, Aida was always there
in the background.

The two lovers could not help looking at each other.

Amneris saw it, and jealousy filled her heart.

But she managed to keep it hidden... for now.

**KEY WORDS**

- background
- cannot help -ing
- jealousy

- manage to
- hidden
- for now

POP QUIZ
How did Aida feel when Radamès was chosen to be commander?
ⓐ jealous and angry
ⓑ worried and proud

Radamès' thoughts were interrupted by the arrival of the Pharaoh himself.

Many priests and soldiers came with him. Princess Amneris and Aida were there, too.

Everyone gathered at the palace, waiting for news of their enemies.

At last, a messenger arrived. "It's true!" he said.

"The Ethiopians are coming, and their king is leading them."

"Then we need a brave commander," declared the Pharaoh. "Radamès shall lead our army."

The priests and soldiers broke into a song, praising their country and their leaders.

Ramadès was overjoyed. The first part of his dream had already come true!

The people walked with him to the temple, celebrating all the way.

But Aida remained alone in the palace, her feelings too much for her to bear.

She was proud of Radamès, but also worried for him.

**KEY WORDS**

- interrupt
- **break into** (break-broke-broken)
- praise

- overjoyed
- celebrate

But, to make matters worse, Egypt's great enemy, the
king Amonasro of Ethiopia, was Aida's father!

What was she to think? She loved both men and wanted
them to be safe.

One moment she was praying for the victory of Radamès.
The next, she was longing for her father to win the battle.
There was nothing she could do but hope the gods would
somehow show mercy to them both.

A few days later, the news came that everyone had been waiting for: Radamès was the victor!

The Egyptian army had won the battle against Ethiopia.

Princess Amneris waited in her rooms for Radamès to return.

She commanded her slaves to entertain her while she waited, celebrating his great victory.

But Aida was quiet and thoughtful. She hung back from the celebrations.

Amneris decided to test her and see if she really did love Radamès.

"You may all leave now," she told her slaves, "except Aida. She shall stay with me."

All the other slaves left, leaving the princess and Aida alone together.

"I have some news for you," said Princess Amneris. "It's about Radamès."

The way Aida looked up, hopeful and yet fearful, made the princess angry.

**KEY WORDS**

- to make matters worse
- be + to + *Verb*
- pray for
- long for
- somehow

- victor
- entertain
- thoughtful
- hang back from
  (hang-hung-hung)

- celebration
- hopeful
- fearful

"He is dead!" she declared.

It was a lie, of course, but Aida broke down in tears.

Princess Amneris did not doubt that Aida loved
Radamès. Her jealousy made her angry.

"No, he is not dead. He is alive after all!" she said.

Aida was confused. Was he dead or alive? Should she
weep or dance for joy?

"You love him, don't you?" said the princess. 

"You are my rival for his heart."

Aida couldn't help it — she began to cry again. "Of course I love him."

Princess Amneris' anger turned to fury. She vowed to take her revenge.

She swept out of the room to attend Radamès' victory procession.

It was a grand procession, and Amneris was there to greet the returning hero.

Crowds cheered and sang his praises. The whole of Egypt seemed to be celebrating.

All except one person.

**KEY WORDS**

- break down
- in tears
- doubt
- confused
- rival
- vow
- take one's revenge

- sweep (sweep-swept-swept)
- grand
- procession
- greet
- return
- sing one's praises

Aida had crept out of the palace to watch the procession.
A long line of Ethiopian prisoners trailed after the
victorious army. Her father, King Amonasro, was among
them.

Relief rushed over Aida that at least he was still alive,
even though he was a prisoner.

She hurried over to see him, but King Amonasro shook
his head at her.

"No one knows who I am," he said. "They think I am
just another soldier.

They must not know that I am the king, nor that you
and I are related."
The Pharaoh was delighted with Radamès.
"This man shall have anything he asks for," he
announced. "I will honor his victory by granting his
request."

Then, he turned his attention to the enemy prisoners.

"Who will speak for you? I must decide what shall be done with you."

Amonasro stepped forward. He didn't look like a king, with no crown or royal robes.

He looked just like the rest of the Ethiopian people.

Their black skin protected them from the burning Egyptian sun, but not from the Pharaoh.

"The king of Ethiopia is dead," Amonasro announced.
"He was killed in battle. You are the victors and you have nothing more to lose. Please pardon us and let us go."

"No!" The crowd didn't like this idea.

They roared their protest. "Don't let our enemies go."

"Kill every Ethiopian within our land!"

The Pharaoh nodded and said, "Very well."

He didn't want to go against the wishes of his people.

They might rise up against him and put someone new on the throne.

Radamès listened, horrified, to their chanting.

If all the Ethiopians were killed, then his beloved Aida would be, too!

## KEY WORDS

- turn one's attention
- speak for
- forward
- crown
- robe
- rest
- protect
- pardon
- roar
- protest
- nod
- go against
- wish
- rise up against
- chant
- beloved

"Pharaoh, I have thought about my request," he called
out in a loud voice.

"I know that you are a generous man and that you will
honor your promise to grant me whatever I ask.
Please do not kill these prisoners, but set them free."
The Pharaoh thought for a while, and then agreed.
"Our enemies may go free, but I will keep this man as a
prisoner." He pointed at Amonasro.
"Then the other Ethiopians will keep their word and will
not attack us again.
My daughter's slave, Aida, is to stay in the city, too. She
shall not have her freedom."
Radamès was partly relieved. Aida would live!
But he was also dismayed, because he still could not
marry her.

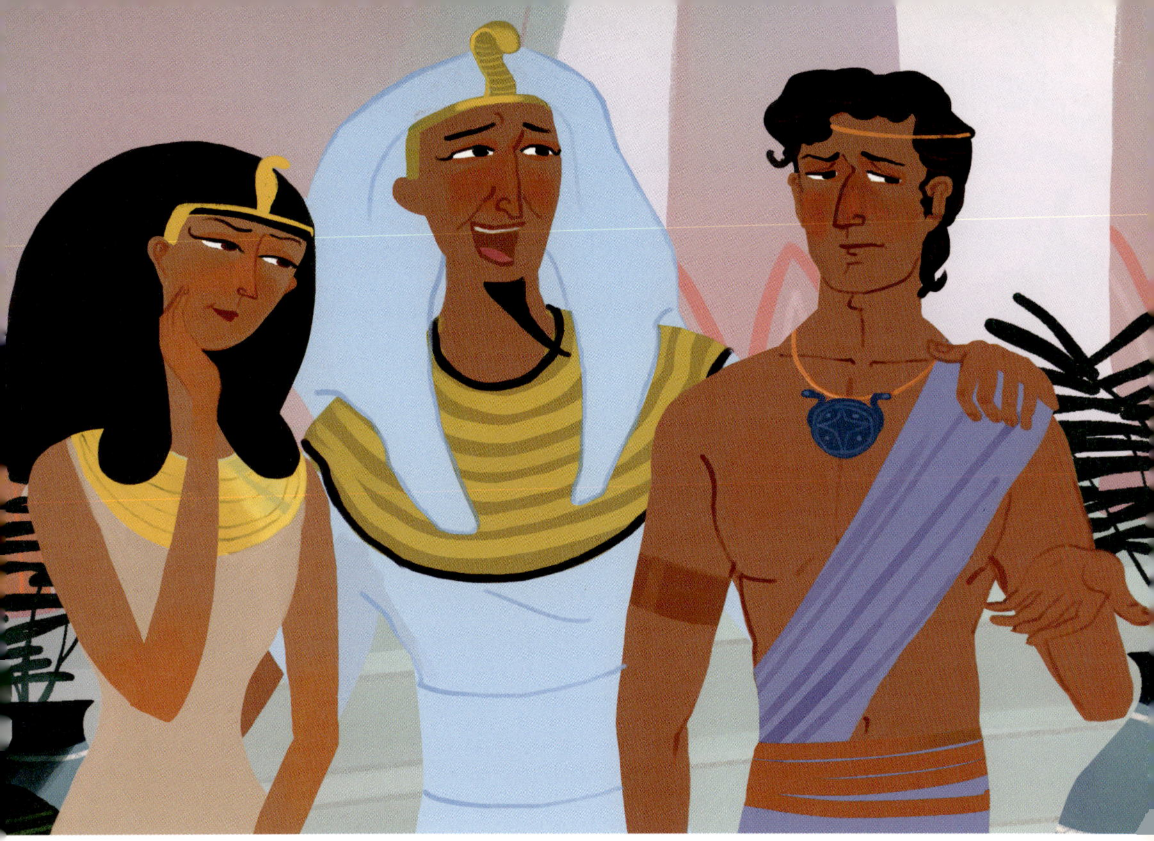

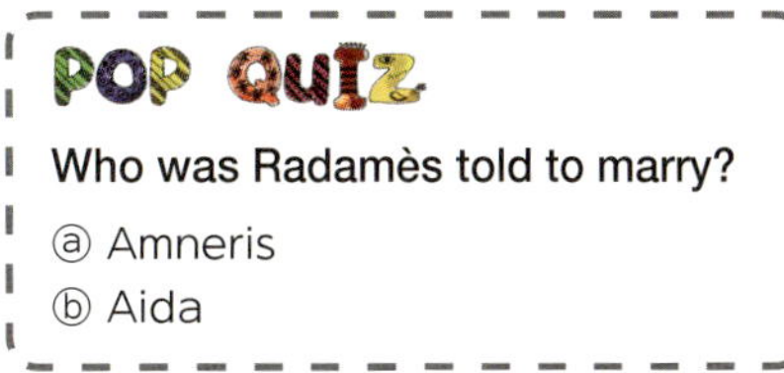

He was even more horrified at what the Pharaoh said next.

"As a victor's reward, Radamès shall marry my daughter, Princess Amneris.

When I die, he shall rule all of Egypt alongside her."

**POP QUIZ**

Who was Radamès told to marry?

ⓐ Amneris

ⓑ Aida

**A** Who might say each line? Match each line with the person who is likely to say it.

❶ I serve in the temple. I warned Radamès that the Ethiopians were coming.

❷ My daughter serves the princess. I am a king, but I came to Egypt disguised as an ordinary man.

❸ I am in love with Radamès. I am jealous because my slave loves him too.

a) 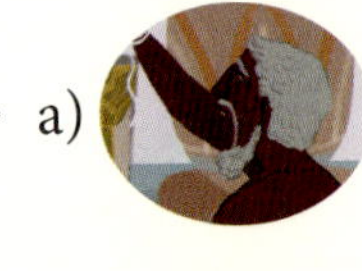

b) 

c) 

**B** Mark T for true or F for false.

❶ The king of Ethiopia was killed in the battle.　T　F

❷ Amonasro wore a crown and royal robes.　T　F

❸ Most of the Ethiopians were set free.　T　F

❹ The Egyptians wanted the Pharaoh to kill all the Ethiopians.　T　F

  Choose the best answer to each question.

❶ Why couldn't Radamès tell everyone that he loved Aida?

   a) He was already married to Amneris.

   b) He was not allowed to marry a slave.

   c) He was ashamed of himself for loving her.

   d) He was a soldier, and soldiers were not allowed to marry at all.

❷ What did Radamès ask the Pharaoh for?

   a) He asked for permission to marry Aida.

   b) He asked for permission to marry Princess Amneris.

   c) He asked for the power to rule over Egypt.

   d) He asked for all the Ethiopian prisoners to be set free.

**D**  Fill in each blank with the right word below.

| reason | prize | victory | dream |
|---|---|---|---|

❶ Radamès wanted to lead his troops to ____________.

❷ There was another ____________ why Radamès wanted to win the battle.

❸ He hoped that his ____________ might come true.

❹ Aida would be the ____________ that Radamès hoped for.

# Chapter Two

# Deadly Decisions

It was the eve of the wedding.

The next day, Amneris and Radamès would be husband and wife! Aida was full of despair.

She waited outside the temple, keeping to the shadows and hoping that nobody would see her.

Radamès had managed to speak to her privately, in a snatched moment when the princess wasn't looking. They had arranged to meet here. But Aida did not know what he wanted to say to her.

"Will he tell me that all is lost?" she wondered.

"If so, I cannot bear it.

I would rather throw myself in the River Nile than live without him."

**POP QUIZ**

**When did the events of this chapter take place?**

ⓐ the day after the wedding
ⓑ the day before the wedding

**KEY WORDS**

- deadly
- decision
- eve
- despair

- keep to
- privately
- snatch
- arrange

Someone was coming!

She pressed herself against the wall and held her breath.

Princess Amneris and the priest, Ramfis, approached.

But they didn't see Aida. Instead, they went into the temple to pray.

Aida got lost in thought once more.

"If Radamès does not love me, I will never again see my homeland.

I will never turn my face to its blue skies and cool valleys, I will never see its green hills and beautiful beaches."

Someone else was coming!

This time, it was Aida's father, Amonasro.

Somehow, he had managed to escape from the guards that watched over him.

"I have heard that the Egyptian army will go and invade Ethiopia," he said.

"You must remain loyal to me and to your country.
When Radamès comes, find out from him which way
the army will go.
Then our people will be ready to fight, and we will not
be defeated again."

What was Aida to do?

She did not want to betray Radamès and ruin his battle plans. But neither did she want to betray her father.

This time when she heard footsteps approaching, it really was Radamès.

Amonasro hid nearby as Radamès rushed to meet Aida.

"My sweet Aida," Radamès said, taking her hand.

"Am I really your sweet Aida?" she asked. "You are going to marry the princess tomorrow, after all. Run away with me instead! We can be happy together in another land, far away from here."

"What? Shall I leave my post as army commander, and all the glory that I have here?"

Radamès was doubtful, but Aida continued to urge him until at last he agreed.

"I love you," he said.  "I will not marry the princess tomorrow. We will leave this place and run away to the desert. There, we will wander under the stars."

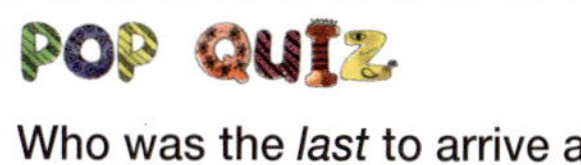



**Who was the *last* to arrive at the temple?**
ⓐ Radamès
ⓑ Amonasro

**KEY WORDS**

- betray
- ruin
- footstep
- **hide** (hide-hid-hidden)
- nearby
- rush to
- run away

- post
- glory
- doubtful
- urge
- desert
- wander

Aida took a deep breath, remembering what her father had asked her.

"But how will we escape the soldiers?" she asked.

"Which way will they go?"

Radamès explained everything to Aida.

He told her which way the soldiers would go when they tried to attack Ethiopia.

Just as he finished speaking, Amonasro stepped out of the shadows.

"Thank you for such useful information," he said, bowing. "The king of Ethiopia is very grateful."

"The king...of Ethiopia...is you? Oh, what have I done? I have betrayed my country." Filled with desperation and guilt, Radamès began to pace up and down.

**What was Radamès guilty of?**

ⓐ betraying his country
ⓑ betraying Aida

**KEY WORDS**

- take a deep breath
- useful
- information
- grateful
- desperation

- guilt
- pace up and down
- calm down
- military
- in the presence of

"Calm down," said Aida. "Everything will be all right."

"I can't calm down! I have told you a military secret in the presence of our greatest enemy."

Amonasro tried to calm him too. But it was too late. The noise brought Princess Amneris and Ramfis, the priest, out of the temple.

POP QUIZ
Why didn't Radamès manage to escape?
ⓐ He didn't run fast enough.
ⓑ He didn't run at all.

"Run!" Aida twisted out of the reach of Ramfis' grasping hands and managed to escape.

Her father was close behind her as the pair fled from the temple area.

But when Aida looked back, Radamès had not moved.

He stood before the princess and the priest, head bowed in shame.

"He has given himself up," whispered Aida to herself.

Her heart was filled with a heaviness that she could not bear.

Sometime later, Radamès was waiting for his trial. He had betrayed his country.

He was a guilty man.

Soldiers guarded him, but he had no will to run away anywhere.

He believed that Aida had been killed.

His life without her was worth nothing.

**KEY WORDS**

- twist
- out of reach
- grasp
- pair
- **flee** (flee-fled-fled)
- in shame

- give oneself up
- heaviness
- trial
- guilty
- will
- worth nothing

Suddenly, the guards stood to attention.

Princess Amneris had arrived!

They allowed her in to see the prisoner.

"What have you done?" she murmured. "You will surely die for your crime."

"I don't care," answered Radamès. "I will gladly die so that I can be with my love, Aida."

"But Aida is not dead."

Radamès' head jolted up. "What do you mean?"

"She escaped, along with her father." Princess Amneris paced around the room like a cat stalking her prey.

"I can make sure that you are pardoned, you know. But I will only do it if you give up this ridiculous love for my slave."

"Never!" Radamès was overjoyed that Aida was still alive.

He was determined that he would stay true to her. But at the same time, he knew that he could not escape his fate.

**POP QUIZ**

**Why was Radamès happy?**

ⓐ He knew that Aida was still alive.

ⓑ He knew that Aida had planned his escape.

**KEY WORDS**

- stand to attention
- crime
- gladly
- jolt up
- pace around
- stalk

- prey
- pardon
- ridiculous
- determined
- stay true to
- fate

Later that day, the soldiers escorted Radamès to his trial.

Princess Amneris followed them.

Radamès stood before the priests as they accused him of betraying his country.

"What will you say to defend yourself?" a priest asked.

But Radamès stayed silent.

"Then we condemn you to be buried alive," he said, solemnly.

"No! Please have mercy, I beg you!" Amneris threw herself on the floor in front of the priests.

"Please change your verdict."

But the priests would not change their minds.

They ordered the soldiers to take Radamès and to seal him into an underground vault below the temple, never to be released.

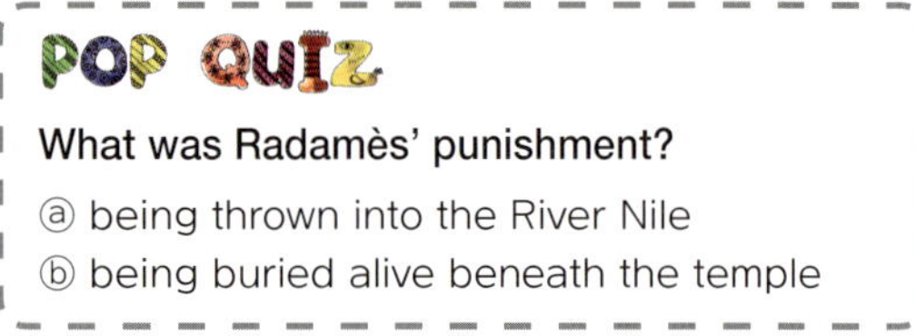


**KEY WORDS**

- escort
- accuse A of B
- defend
- condemn
- bury alive

- solemnly
- throw oneself
- verdict
- seal
- underground vault

- release
- cradle
- run out
- breathe

Inside the vault, Radamès sat down, cradling his head in his hands.

He knew that the air in the vault would soon run out.

Then, he would not be able to breathe.

But he was proud that he had done the right thing in the end.

He was sorry that he had betrayed his country, but at least he had remained faithful to Aida.

He jumped as a figure stepped out of the darkness.

She was barely visible, her skin the same color as the shadows.

"Radamès?" she whispered. "I slipped out when the princess wasn't watching. You will not die alone."

"Aida!" They embraced and kissed one another, declaring their love over and over again.

At last they would be united in death.

They rested for the last time in each other's arms while Amneris, in the temple above, prayed for Radamès' soul.

**KEY WORDS**

- in the end
- jump
- figure
- darkness
- visible
- slip out

- over and over again
- embrace
- be united
- for the last time
- in each other's arms
- soul

POP QUIZ

Why did Aida come to Radames?

ⓐ To die with Radames
ⓑ To help Radames escape

**A** Who might say each line? Match each line with the person who is likely to say it.

❶ Radamès does not love me, but I will try to win his heart.

❷ If I hide in the vault, I will at least see Radamès one more time.

❸ Why did I ever ask him to tell me the military secret?

❹ I should have been married today.

a) 

b) 

**B** Circle the right word for each underlined part.

❶ Aida hid in the (trees / shadows / rooms) outside the (river / palace / temple).

❷ If Radamès told Aida that all was (lost / found / wonderful), she would throw herself in the (fire / river / desert).

❸ When someone came, Aida pressed herself against the (wall / ground / tree) and held her (hand / breath / nose).

❹ Aida missed the blue (hills / beaches / skies) and green (skies / trees / hills) of her homeland.

Solve the crossword puzzle.

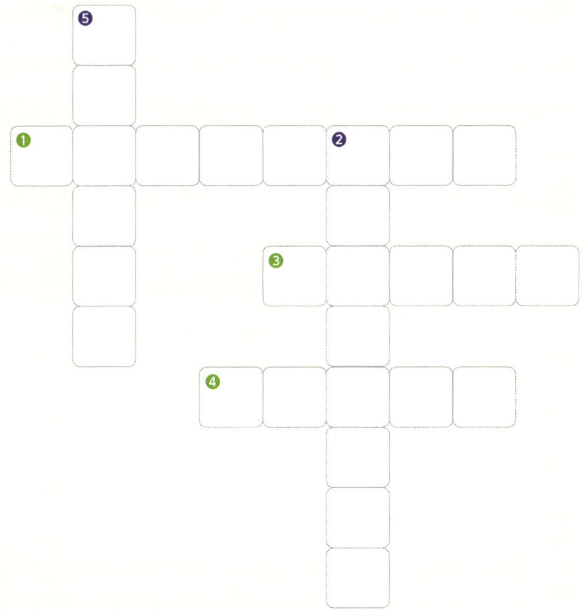

**Across**

❶ The king of Ethiopia was called __________.

❸ Aida was the __________ of Amneris.

❹ Radamès had to face a __________ for what he had done.

**Down**

❷ Radamès was guarded by some __________.

❺ Radamès was put into a vault below the __________.

# Let's Review the Story

Fill in the blanks to review the story.

**Story 1:** T______

Setting (what country?):

C______

Main Characters:

T______ , C______

Other named characters:

T______ , L______ ,
P______ , P______ ,
P______

Main Problem:

C______ wants to marry
T______ . She doesn't want
to m______ anyone.

Solution:

Calaf guesses T______'s
r______ and earns the
right to marry her.

**Story 2:** A______

Setting (what country?):

E______

Main Characters:

A______ , R______

Other named characters:

A______ , R______ ,
A______

Main Problem:

R______ wants to marry
A______ . They are not
allowed to m______ because
Aida is a s______ .

Solution:

Radamès and Aida spend their
l______ moments
t______ .

**Think about the following questions and answer them freely.**

❶ Leaving word that Princess would also know the rapture of love, Liù killed herself. After that, Calàf kissed Turandot and Princess began to weep. What did the tears mean?

❷ Aida stole military secret from her beloved Radamès for her country. Radamès was tormented by the fact and was killed eventually. Was Aida's behavior appropriate? Share your thoughts with your friends.

❸ What touching love stories do you know? Share unobtainable love stories, love stories that overcome the crisis etc. with your friends.

# Let's Review the Story

**Story 1:** Turandot

**Setting (what country?):**
China

**Main Characters:**
Turandot , Calaf

**Other named characters:**
Timur , Liu ,
Ping , Pang ,
Pong

**Main Problem:**
Calaf wants to marry Turandot . She doesn't want to marry anyone.

**Solution:**
Calaf guesses Turandot 's riddles and earns the right to marry her.

**Story 2:** Aida

**Setting (what country?):**
Egypt

**Main Characters:**
Aida , Radamès

**Other named characters:**
Amonasro , Ramfis ,
Amneris

**Main Problem:**
Radamès wants to marry Aida . They are not allowed to marry because Aida is a slave .

**Solution:**
Radamès and Aida spend their last moments together .

# After-reading Test

- Turandot / Aida
- Level 4
- 26 Questions

  (Vocabulary 4 / Reading Comprehension 16 /

  Sentence Structure & Grammar 6)

1.  What does "frail" mean in the following sentence?

    Timur's <u>frail</u> voice called out.

    ① strong
    ② loud
    ③ weak
    ④ fast

2.  What does "reign" mean in the following sentence?

    Who can stop her terrible <u>reign</u>?

    ① a type of weather
    ② a leather strap used to control a horse
    ③ a period of ruling
    ④ a bad temper

3.  What does "urgent" mean in the following sentence?

    Outside the palace, two men were having an <u>urgent</u> conversation.

    ① quiet, spoken in a slow manner
    ② important, requiring immediate attention
    ③ dangerous for others to know
    ④ hard to understand

4. What does "urge" mean in the following sentence?

> Radamès was doubtful, but Aida continued to urge him until at last he agreed.

① encourage
② beat
③ hold
④ entertain

5. How did Giuseppe Verdi learn to compose music?
① He learned it from his grandfather.
② He learned it at school.
③ He learned it from another composer.
④ He learned it by listening to operas.

6. What was the relationship between Timur and Liu?
① husband and wife
② father and daughter
③ brother and sister
④ master and servant

7. Why did NOT Calaf want his name spoken aloud?
① He was embarrassed about his name.
② He did not want his enemies to know that he was in Peking.
③ He did not want Turandot to know who he was.
④ He wanted Liu to guess his name.

8. Who did NOT try to stop Calaf from beating the gong?
  ① Turandot
  ② Liu
  ③ Timur
  ④ Ping, Pong and Pang

9. Why did NOT the Emperor want Calaf to try to answer the riddles?
  ① He didn't want Calaf to die.
  ② He didn't want Calaf to marry his daughter.
  ③ He didn't want Calaf to make Turandot look foolish.
  ④ He didn't want Calaf to enter the palace.

10. Why did NOT Turandot like men?
  ① Men called her unkind names.
  ② She had never spoken to a man.
  ③ A man had killed her ancestor.
  ④ Lots of men tried to make her obey them.

11. Why did Turandot's cheeks flush redder, and why did she tremble?
  ① She was ill.
  ② She was tired.
  ③ She was excited.
  ④ She was angry.

12. Why did Turandot look stern each time Calaf guessed an answer correctly?
① She did not want him to guess correctly.
② She thought that he was cheating.
③ She was angry that a crowd was watching.
④ She was trying not to laugh.

13. What did Radamès hope for? Choose two answers.
① to marry Aida
② to become the Pharaoh
③ to capture slaves
④ to lead the Egyptian army

14. Why was Aida in Egypt?
① She had chosen to come and work for the princess.
② She had come to buy food and she had decided to stay.
③ She had been born into an Egyptian family.
④ She had been captured as a slave and made to serve the princess.

15. Why did NOT Aida celebrate at Radamès' victory procession?
① She believed that Radamès was dead.
② She didn't love Radamès any longer.
③ She was upset by the trick that Amneris had played on her.
④ She saw her father among the prisoners.

16. What happened to Aida when the Ethiopians were released?
    ① She had to stay in the city as a slave.
    ② She was set free with the other prisoners.
    ③ She was given permission to marry Radamès.
    ④ She ran back to her own country.


17. What did Amneris say that Radamès must do if he wanted to go free?
    ① tell her where Amonasro was
    ② marry her at once
    ③ find out when the Ethiopian army would attack
    ④ give up his love for Aida


18. What did Amonasro want Aida to find out from Radamès?
    ① whether or not he would marry the princess
    ② whether the Pharaoh might let him go home
    ③ which way the Egyptian army might go
    ④ what sort of weapons Radamès would use to attack Ethiopia


19. Why did Radamès feel guilty when Amonasro appeared?
    ① He should not have been talking to Aida.
    ② He should not have given away a military secret.
    ③ He should not have been standing near the temple.
    ④ He should not have agreed to leave his country.

20. Why did Aida hide in the vault?
　① She was planning to help Radamès to escape.
　② She didn't want to watch the wedding.
　③ She wanted to kill herself so that Radamès would go free.
　④ She wanted to die with Radamès.

21. Choose the wrong part of the sentence.

> She was not barely visible.
> 　①　②　③　　④

※ Choose the correct word or phrase for each blank. (22~24)

22.
> Princess Turandot ordered that Liu __________ punished.

　① was
　② had been
　③ must be
　④ could be

23.
> The princess, __________ had never been kissed before, began to weep.

　① which　　　　　　　② who
　③ why　　　　　　　④ when

24.

> He had managed to ___________ from the guards that watched over him.

① escape

② escapes

③ escaping

④ escaped

※ Choose the correct sentence. (25~26)

25. ① You love him, are you?

    ② You love him, aren't you?

    ③ You love him, do you?

    ④ You love him, don't you?

26. ① Too much blood has spilled already.

    ② Too much blood has been spilled already.

    ③ Too much blood have spilled already.

    ④ Too much blood have been spilled already.

**Sarah J. Dodd**

Sarah J. Dodd is an experienced primary school teacher who resides in the UK, but has also lived and taught in Australia. She has a PhD in Science and a certificate in Creative Writing. She has published several books for children: "An Angel Anyway" (Anyway Press, 2008) the "Little Angels" series (Lion Children's Books, 2009/10), "The Lion Picture Bible" (Lion Children's Books, 2015) and "Legs: the tale of a meerkat lost and found" (Lion Children's Books, 2015). Her poetry for children has also been highly commended and published in the anthology "Let in the Stars" (Manchester Metropolitan University, 2014).

She is currently working on further picture books for the very young, and a novel for older children.

# Turandot / Aida


Retold by Sarah J. Dodd
Illustrated by Juyeon Kim

First Published in July 2015

Editorial Manager: Juyon Choi
Editors: Juyon Choi, Hyunjung Kim, Kyunghee Jang, Jiyeong Park
Designers: Eunhee Lee, Elim
Cover Designer: Eunhee Lee

Published and distributed by

Darakwon Bldg., 64-1 Jandari-ro, Mapo-gu, Seoul, Korea 121-894
Tel: 82-2-736-2031(ext. 250)    Fax: 82-2-732-2037
Homepage: www.ihappyhouse.co.kr
Publisher: Kyudo Chung





ISBN: 978-89-6653-201-8 18740 / 978-89-6653-156-1 18740(set)

[Components]
• 1 Audio CD (Recording Studio: Aram)
• Answer Keys & Korean Translation: Free download at www.ihappyhouse.co.kr